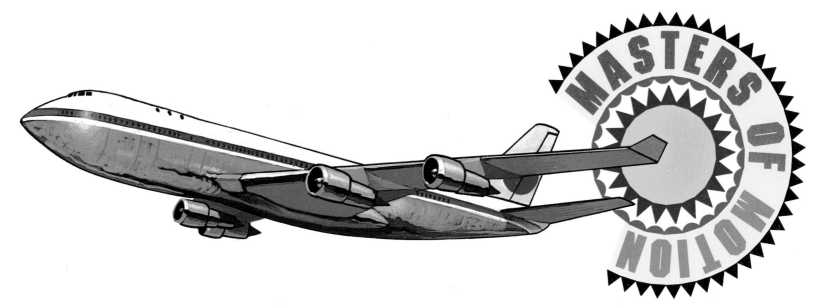

# MASTERS OF MOTION

# HOW TO FLY A 747

## TIM PAULSON

ILLUSTRATED BY GREGORY TRUETT SMITH, JIM FINNELL, AND CHRIS BRIGMAN
PHOTOGRAPHY BY EDWARD KEATING

John Muir Publications, P.O. Box 613, Santa Fe, NM 87504

Text ©1992 by Agincourt Press
Cover and interior illustrations ©1992 by John Muir Publications
All rights reserved. Published 1992
Printed in the United States of America

First edition. First printing September 1992

Library of Congress Cataloging-in-Publication Data
Paulson, Tim
    How to fly a 747 / Tim Paulson ; photography by Edward Keating ;
  illustrated by Gregory Truett Smith, James Finnell, and Chris Brigman. —
  1st ed.
      p. cm. — (Masters of Motion)
    Includes index.
    Summary: Places the reader at the controls of a 747 jumbo jet and
  introduces the principles of aerodynamics while moving step by step
  through preflight, takeoff, flight, and landing.
    ISBN 1-56261-061-9 (pbk.)  $9.95
  1. Jet planes—Piloting—Juvenile literature. 2. Boeing 747
  (Jet transports)—Juvenile literature. [1. Jet planes—Piloting.]
  I. Keating, Edward, ill. II. Smith, Gregory Truett, ill.
  III. Finnell, Jim, ill.  IV. Title.  V. Series.
  TL710.P37  1992
  629.132'5216—dc20
                                    91-48222
                                      CIP
                                      AC

Consultants: Agincourt Press
Design: Ken Wilson
Illustrations: James Finnell, Gregory Truett Smith, Chris Brigman
Typography: Ken Wilson
Printer: Worzalla
Photographs by Edward Keating,except photographs on pages 5,8 (top),
8-9, 12-13, and 36 courtesy of Boeing.


Distributed to the book trade by
W. W. Norton, Inc.
New York, New York


Distributed to the education market by
The Wright Group
19201 120th Avenue NE
Bothell, WA  98011

## ACKNOWLEDGMENTS

We would like to thank Jim Waugh, Sr., Jim Waugh, Jr., and Chuck Carlson for their active and generous support of this project.

BOEING and 747 are trademarks of the Boeing Company.

Wait a second! Where am I? I'm looking down on the clouds! And what are all these lights and gauges in front of me? How weird. I'm actually at the controls of a 747, soaring 41,000 feet above the ground! How do you fly one of these things?

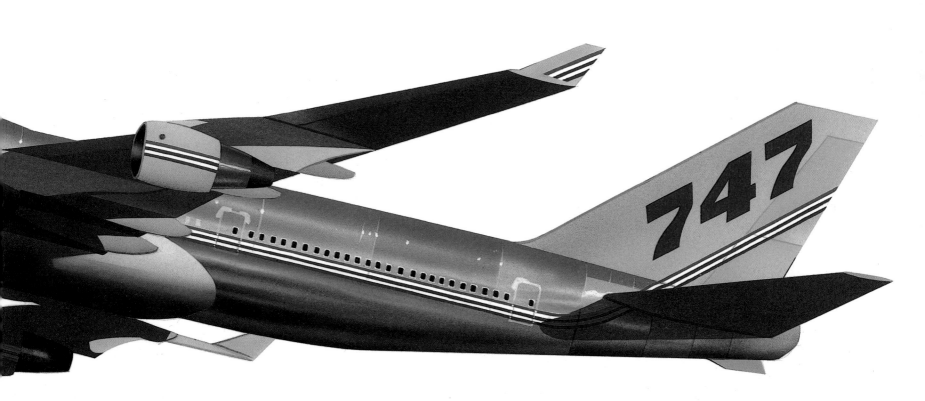

The controls on a 747 are designed to be read at a glance. They are arranged like spokes around a wheel, with the most important controls at the hub, directly in front of the pilot.

*Ah ha! Headphones. Maybe I can reach someone on the radio.*

You don't need to do that. I'll be happy to help you out.

*"Who said that?"*

I did. I'm Chuck. I'm sitting right behind you—in what we call the jump seat. I'm an expert 747 pilot, and I'm here to help you fly this bird. Just pay attention, and I'll teach you everything you need to know.

For instance, did you know that this is the largest commercial aircraft in the world? I mean this bird is BIG! It's got enough wing area to hold a full-size basketball court, and it's long, too. They say the Wright brothers' first flight at Kitty Hawk could have taken place entirely within the coach cabin.

*"No, I didn't know that. But what about flying the plane? Where do I start?"*

Why not at the beginning? It looks like there's an airport below us, so why don't I just take us down, and then you can find out how to fly a 747—from takeoff right through to landing.

## ON THE GROUND

Now that we're on the ground, it's time for you to learn some of the principles of flight. Once you learn how flight works, it'll be much easier for you to understand how the controls of a 747 work.

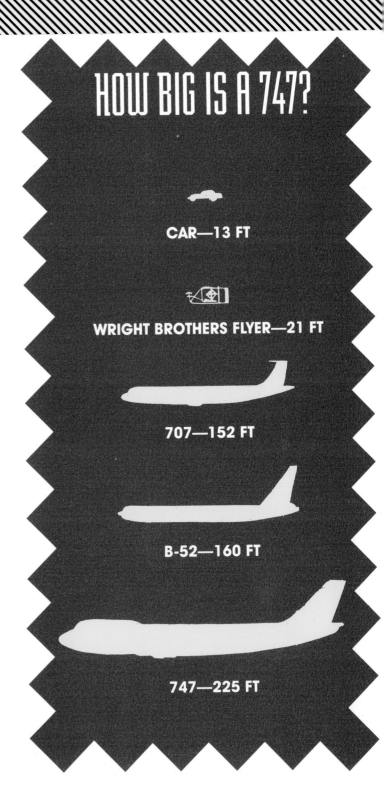

# HOW BIG IS A 747?

CAR—13 FT

WRIGHT BROTHERS FLYER—21 FT

707—152 FT

B-52—160 FT

747—225 FT

Basically, to fly you have to achieve lift, an upward force that overcomes the downward pull of gravity. A typical plane does this by using its engines to generate thrust. This thrust propels the plane forward—which, in turn, causes air to flow quickly past the wings. Because none of the air can go through the wings, some air goes over them and some air goes under them. As engine thrust increases, so does the plane's speed, and so does the speed of the wind flowing past the wings.

Now look carefully at the shape of each wing. Do you see how they are curved on top but flat underneath? That shape is crucial, because it means that air flowing over the wings has to travel farther than air flowing under them. Are you with me so far?

*"Sure. The wind above the wing has to travel farther. So what?"*

Here's where we get a little assist from the laws of physics. One of these laws states that air will always try to stay in equilibrium, or in balance, with itself. This means that the air flowing over the wing will always try to keep up with, or stay in equilibrium with, the air flowing under the wing.

*"But the air flowing over the wing has to travel farther . . ."*

So, to keep up, it also has to travel faster. And that's where lift comes in. The fact that the air above the wing has to move faster than the air beneath the wing causes a difference in pressure, or a pressure differential. It's as though the air above the wing is stretched

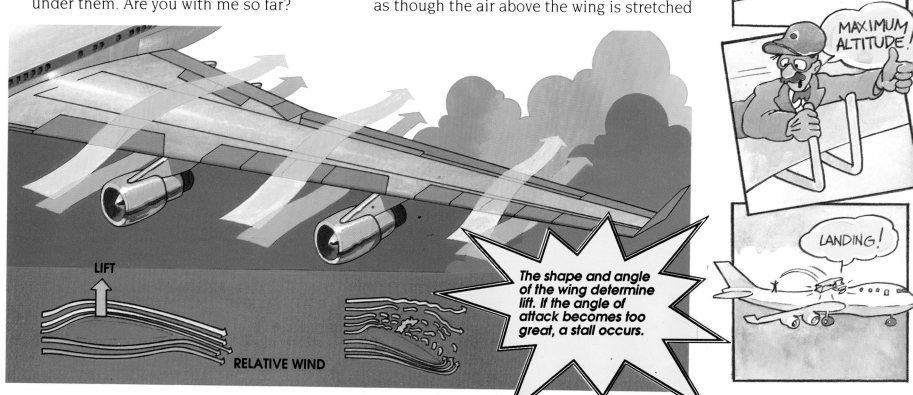

LIFT

RELATIVE WIND

The shape and angle of the wing determine lift. If the angle of attack becomes too great, a stall occurs.

READY?

READY!

TAKE OFF!!!

MAXIMUM ALTITUDE!

LANDING!

out. Because it's moving faster, there's less of it in a given space and therefore less pressure above the wing than below it.

This difference in pressure is the lift. The low-pressure area above the wing pulls the plane up like a vacuum, while the high pressure area below the wing helps out with a push. About 75 percent of the lift comes from the pull and about 25 percent from the push.

*"Does the speed of the plane matter?"*

Of course it does, because the speed of the plane directly affects the speed of the air flowing past the wings, which is called the relative wind. The faster a plane moves through the air, the greater the difference in pressure, and the greater the lift.

Something called the "angle of attack" also affects lift. This is the angle between the wing and the relative wind. As the wing tilts up and the angle of attack increases, more air is concentrated under the wing. This increases the pressure differential and therefore the lift.

*This analog tachometer gives the 747's airspeed, in knots. There is also a digital speed indicator.*

*"This is getting a bit complicated."*

Think of it this way: You're in a convertible, holding your hand palm down as though it

# ANGLE OF ATTACK

CENTER LINE OF PLANE

ANGLE OF ATTACK

WING CHORD LINE

PRIMARY FLIGHT
DISPLAY

THROTTLE

EICAS DISPLAY
SELECT PANEL

NAVIGATION
DISPLAY

EICAS

**MAIN PANEL**

were a wing. At low speeds, you don't feel much. But as the car accelerates and the relative wind gets stronger, it becomes harder and harder to keep your hand still. Your hand keeps wanting to move up or down depending on the angle at which it meets the wind.

Wings are designed to take advantage of these same forces, and the angle of attack is one of the means by which a pilot controls them. Of course, the forces that act on a 747 are a lot more powerful than the wind you feel in a car. But that's understandable. After all, it takes an awful lot of lift to get 870,000 pounds of jet off the ground.

*"I think I've got it now. Wings are rounded on top so that the air will have to flow faster over them than under them. And because fast air means less pressure, you get lift."*

That's basically it. But we've got to move fast now because the tower has just cleared us for takeoff in less than two minutes.

*"That doesn't give us much time."*

I'll talk fast. The cockpit you're sitting in has been very carefully designed so that every control you need is within easy reach. But it wasn't always this way. In the original 747s, there were nearly a thousand switches, lights, and dials spread all over the cockpit. There were so many controls, in fact, that not even the pilot and the copilot together could reach them all, so there had to be a third person in the cockpit crew. But now, on the latest model—the 747-400—there are only 365 controls, down from 971, and they're easily handled by a crew of two. This cockpit may look complicated to a civilian, but to the average pilot of a few years back, it looks almost empty.

*"What happened to all the extra dials and knobs and switches?"*

Most were replaced by the automation, others by engineering and design improvements.

*"So the autopilot can do just about everything?"*

It can do a lot—but not everything. It can't take off, for instance. Only a human pilot can do that.

*"Speaking of taking off, isn't it about time I learned how?"*

Right. Taking off. You need two things: speed and lift. And, really, the speed gives you the lift. To get the speed, you use these four engines here, two on each of the wings.

**On takeoff, the throttle handles must all be pulled back together.**

# WATCH THAT ATTITUDE

A plane's attitude is described in terms of its pitch, yaw, and roll. Pitch is the degree to which either the nose or the tail is pointing up. Yaw refers to the flatwise twist of the plane—that is, whether the nose is pointing to the pilot's right or left. And roll describes the spin of the plane along the axis of the fuselage, much the way a hot dog spins on a spit.

Different control surfaces work together to control the plane's attitude. Pitch is controlled by the elevators on the tail, yaw by the tail rudder, and roll by the ailerons. For any of these control surfaces to work, however, the plane has to be moving forward quite fast, because deflecting air doesn't mean much unless the force of the air being deflected is quite strong itself.

**YAW**          **ROLL**          **PITCH**

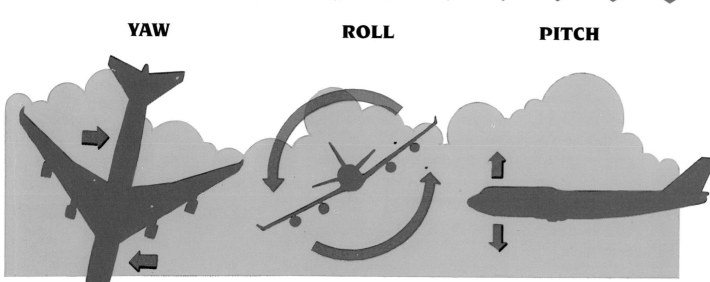

Look at the throttle controls. See how each engine is controlled by an individually numbered lever? But the levers are also grouped together so that you can power all four engines at once for an even thrust.

On takeoff, we also extend the flaps, which are movable extensions of the wings. They add a bit to the drag but increase the total wing area, and that gives us more lift. Flaps make it possible for the plane to take off quickly, at slower runway speeds, which helps a lot on short runways.

*"How will I know when I'm going fast enough to take off?"*

Directly in front of you is a little TV screen called the Primary Flight Display, or PFD for short. It shows you all the important information you need for flight. Those sideways L's in the center section represent the wings as seen from behind. They show the plane's attitude—in this case, its roll, or how level it is. To the right is the navigation display. Below is the altitude gauge, which tells you the barometric altitude, or the height above sea level. There's also another instrument that gives us the height of the landing gear in feet above the ground.

*"What does all that have to do with takeoff speed?"*

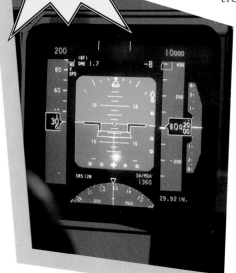

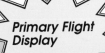
**There is one throttle lever for each of the four engines.**

**Primary Flight Display**

There are always four forces working on a plane: lift, weight, thrust, and drag. Lift, or the upward force generated by the wings, causes the plane to climb whenever lift exceeds weight, or the downward force generated by gravity. Thrust creates forward momentum. Drag works passively against thrust, just as gravity works passively against lift.

The drag created by a plane's movement through air is called parasite drag because it has no other purpose than the unwanted effect of slowing the plane down. There are three types of parasite drag: form drag, skin friction, and interference drag. Form drag comes from the inevitable fact that hitting oncoming air always slows an object down. It's the same resistance you feel running against the wind. On a plane, form drag is caused by the form of the plane itself—the fuselage, wings, engines, antennas, and all the other parts of the plane that come in contact with the air.

Skin friction is the loss of energy that occurs whenever two surfaces rub together. In a car, the friction between the tires and the road is what causes a car to slow down even without applying the brakes. In flight, the corresponding friction is that between the air and the metal surfaces of the plane.

Interference drag comes from the pockets of cross-current wind generated by unusual contours on the airplane, such as the point at which the wings join the fuselage or the engines join the wing. Because these intersection points are not aerodynamically efficient, they disrupt the airflow past the plane, much as irregularities along a stream bank create eddies.

Though it's impossible to eliminate drag completely, it's the job of aerospace engineers to come up with new ways that keep this drag to a minimum. Innovations can include more streamlined designs to reduce form and interference drag, as well as smoother surfaces to reduce skin friction. Fighter planes, for instance, experience less form and interference drag because their wings are swept back at an angle.

The reduction of drag is a particularly important aspect of aircraft design because it can dramatically affect fuel consumption. Drag rises exponentially in relation to airspeed. So a plane flying at 200 knots experiences four times the drag encountered by a plane flying at 100 knots. Similarly, tripling airspeed increases drag by nine times. That's why Boeing engineers put the first 747 through 12,000 hours of wind tunnel tests before they found just the right shape.

I'm getting there. Look on the left side of the PFD. See those numbers? You'll see how they spin past the indicator box as we taxi faster. They show our speed. When we begin our takeoff run, those numbers will increase until codes representing the three critical stages of takeoff appear next to the hash mark.

The first takeoff stage is V1. The "V" stands for velocity, or speed. When the plane's speed reaches V1, that means it's too late to abort, or stop, the takeoff, because if you did try to stop, you'd run out of runway before the plane could brake completely. The second stage is VR, or velocity rotation. It's called that because at VR, the nose of the plane rotates up. VR is also called the "unstick" speed,

**FORM DRAG**

**SKIN FRICTION**

**INTERFERENCE DRAG**

LIFT

SCALE

WEIGHT

THRUST

WOOOSH

DRAG

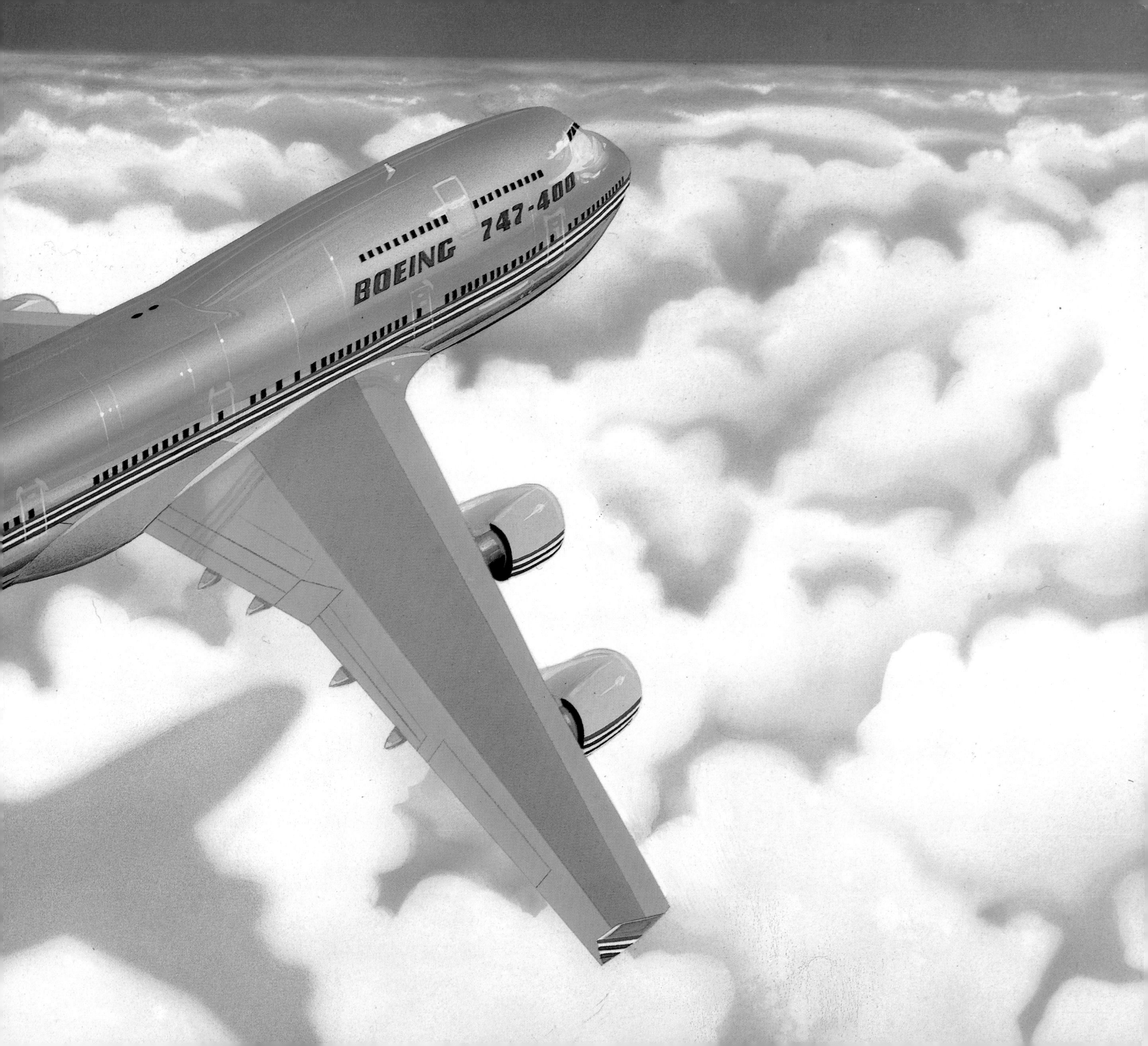
BOEING
747-400

because it's the speed at which the plane becomes "unstuck" from the ground. The third stage is V2. Reaching V2 means that you can lose power in one of your engines and still fly because you're already going fast enough to maintain both lift and control of the plane. But VR is the most important, because it's at VR that you pull back gently on the stick and take off. Got that?"

"At VR, I *pull back on the stick.*"

Right.

"O.K., *what's the stick?*"

The control yoke. You've got your hands on it now.

"*Oh, this thing. I thought it was the steering wheel.*"

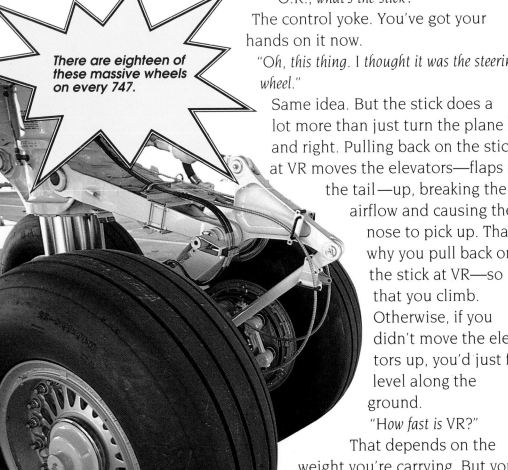

There are eighteen of these massive wheels on every 747.

Same idea. But the stick does a lot more than just turn the plane left and right. Pulling back on the stick at VR moves the elevators—flaps on the tail—up, breaking the airflow and causing the nose to pick up. That's why you pull back on the stick at VR—so that you climb. Otherwise, if you didn't move the elevators up, you'd just fly level along the ground.

"*How fast is VR?*"

That depends on the weight you're carrying. But you can usually count on about 140 knots.

"*Knots?*"

Knots are a measure of speed. The term originally comes from sailing, but we use it in aviation as well. One knot means one nautical mile per hour, and a nautical mile is about 1.15 statute miles.

"*What's a statute mile?*"

A regular mile.

"*So knots are like miles per hour. But 100 knots is a little faster than 100 miles per hour.*"

Right, but let's get back to the takeoff. After you've taxied out onto the runway, you let the engines gather power. Then you release the brakes and really feel the muscle of this plane. From a standing start, the 747 can reach V1 in as little as twenty seconds.

"*That's not much reaction time in case anything goes wrong.*"

No, it's not. But that's why pilots are so well trained. Ready to go?

"*Sure am, Chuck. Let's roll. I know the flaps have to be extended to give me lift, and I know I need to get to VR before I pull back on the stick. That's simple enough. What else is there?*"

Well, you've also got to think about keeping the plane straight as it rolls down the runway.

Fortunately, there's another control surface on the tail of the plane, just above and perpendicular to the elevators. It's called the rudder, and it works just like the rudder on a boat. But instead of moving water, it moves air. The controls for the rudder are those pedals at your feet.

*"So I keep the plane straight with the rudder. What else?"*

Once you start climbing, you should retract the landing gear right away, because unlike the flaps, the landing gear is all drag and no lift. And once you get up to about 1,000 feet, you retract the flaps to reduce the drag even more. Normally, the copilot does this at the command of the pilot, but you may want to try it. The landing gear control is right there in the middle.

*"The lever with the little plastic wheel on it? Cute."*

You pull it up. But remember to wait until you're well clear of the ground.

*"That's it? That's all I need to know to take off?"*

That's about it. You can prepare for takeoff now.

Lowering the elevators on the tail causes the nose to dip. Raising the elevators picks up the nose.

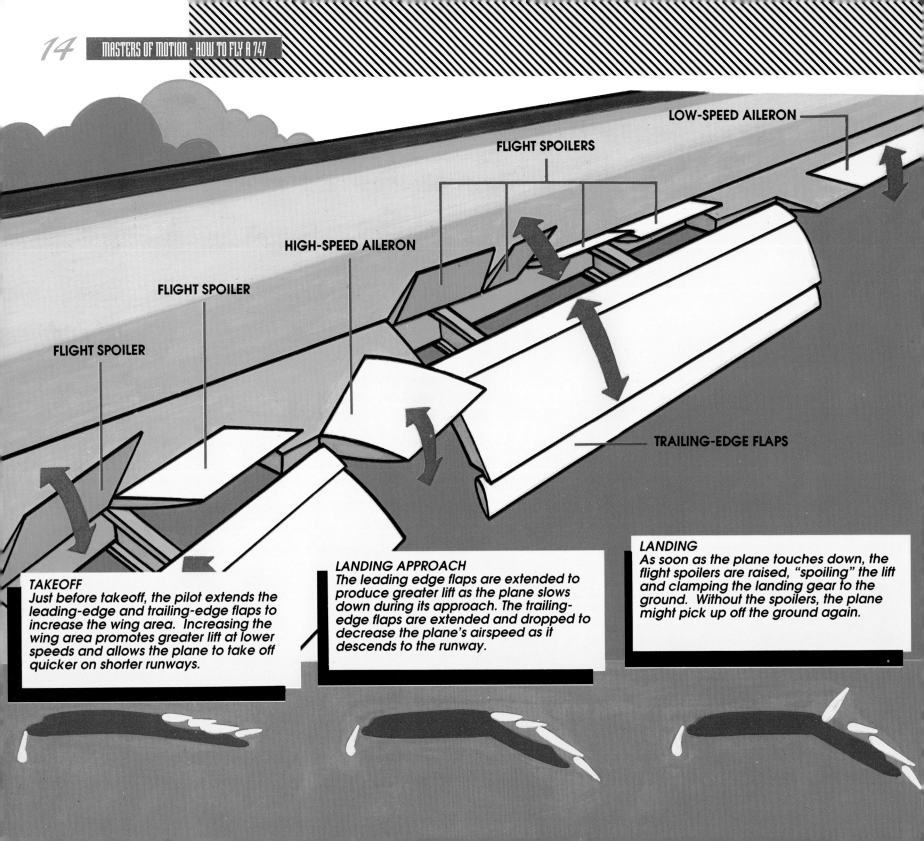

LOW-SPEED AILERON

FLIGHT SPOILERS

HIGH-SPEED AILERON

FLIGHT SPOILER

FLIGHT SPOILER

TRAILING-EDGE FLAPS

**TAKEOFF**
*Just before takeoff, the pilot extends the leading-edge and trailing-edge flaps to increase the wing area. Increasing the wing area promotes greater lift at lower speeds and allows the plane to take off quicker on shorter runways.*

**LANDING APPROACH**
*The leading edge flaps are extended to produce greater lift as the plane slows down during its approach. The trailing-edge flaps are extended and dropped to decrease the plane's airspeed as it descends to the runway.*

**LANDING**
*As soon as the plane touches down, the flight spoilers are raised, "spoiling" the lift and clamping the landing gear to the ground. Without the spoilers, the plane might pick up off the ground again.*

# WINGING IT

Airplane wings can be very simple. In fact, there are only two absolute requirements for a wing: it must be curved on top to generate lift, and it must have a pivoting section called an aileron to help the plane turn. Of course, the 747 wing is much more complex.

Far from being fixed in shape, the wing of a 747 is made up almost entirely of moving panels. To begin with, there are not one but two ailerons on each wing: a low-speed aileron on the outer edge of the wing (for more leverage) and a shorter, high-speed aileron closer to the fuselage. At slower speeds, only the combined force of the two ailerons is enough to turn the plane. But at the fast cruising speeds of the 747, the slight deflection caused by the inboard, high-speed aileron is more than enough to bank it.

In addition to the two ailerons, each 747 wing also has three sets of leading-edge flaps, two sets of trailing-edge flaps, and six spoilers. The flaps work at the command of the pilot to adjust the shape of the wing. Extending the flaps on takeoff and landing increases the wing's ability to generate lift. Retracting them at cruising altitude reduces the plane's drag. In this way, the flap allows the pilot to make the wing bigger or smaller as necessary.

The vertical flight spoilers have a dual function. During a turn, the five outboard spoilers help the ailerons bank the plane. On landings, all six spoilers rise up to break the airflow over the wing and "spoil" the lift.

Seen here from below, this wing must help create enough lift to put 870,000 pounds of plane into the air. Fifteen percent of that weight—56,000 pounds—is in the wings themselves.

Winglets like this one were added to the new, longer 747-400 wings to increase stability in flight. Because special aluminum alloys were used, the new six feet of wing added no extra weight; the light metal used throughout the wing offset the 5,000 pounds of additional weight.

# JETS DO FLAP THEIR WINGS

People generally think of metal as a pretty inflexible substance. And the 747 is certainly made out of metal. But during a typical flight, not one single part of the 747 remains absolutely stiff. The wings, in particular, are almost always in motion, bending gently up and down as small pockets of turbulence buffet them about. In wind tunnels, where this effect can be exaggerated, the wings can actually be made to flap much like a bird's.

And this flexibility is the plane's strength. Because it can bend, the 747 is very tough to break. The wings, for example, are constructed around a 95-foot-long spar. Because each spar arrives at the factory as a single piece, it requires a special truck with an extra steering wheel in the back to transport it. During one routine test, a wing is bent up 35 feet at its tip, at which point it snaps with the sound of a sonic boom!

## PREFLIGHT

"Isn't there some sort of checklist we have to run through?"

You better believe there is. You think I'd let a novice like you go up without checking every system on this plane first? When it comes to flying, there's nothing more important than safety, so pilots always check and double check everything.

System readiness is one of the pilot's most important responsibilities. And remember, a checklist is not the same thing as a do list. Everything on the checklist should already have been done before you check it. And that's not all. Before the checklist is even run through, either the pilot or the copilot does a "walkaround," which means that he or she actually walks around the outside of the plane just in case the instruments are missing something obvious. The walkaround is one of the oldest rituals in aviation, and it's still done just to make sure that everything's in perfect order for flight.

To run through the entire preflight checklist again would take twenty minutes, but there are still a few little details to take care of. This is how we'll handle them: I'll call out each task, and you respond out loud as you accomplish it.

"Why out loud?"

It's called "challenge and response." Pilots always verbalize their checklists rather than run through them mentally, so that they don't just think about something but actually do it.

Speaking out loud also allows the Cockpit Voice Recorder—sometimes called the black box—to record, as much as possible, everything the pilots say and do. The recorder is virtually destruction-proof so that if anything ever goes wrong, experts can review the tape for help in figuring out whether an important step was left out. Of course, the tape is only a thirty-minute loop, but it's those last thirty minutes before an accident that really matter. Also, complete concentration is vital to everyone's safety, and speaking out loud helps most people concentrate.

In discussions of safety, you'll often hear pilots talking about "intrusive interruption." That's when something happens that interferes with the job of flying the plane. Pilots try to avoid intrusive interruptions as much as possible, especially when the plane is below 10,000 feet. That's why we keep what's known as a "sterile cockpit" at low altitudes. No talking about what you had for lunch or dinner or the movie you saw last night. You just think about the plane, only the plane.

*"What's so important about keeping a sterile cockpit below 10,000 feet? Why not 12,000 feet or 20,000?"*

Below 10,000 feet you find a lot of light planes flying around in your airspace. Few of these planes have the kind of sophisticated transponders, or radio transmitters, that warn larger jets of possible collisions, so you have to be very careful when you're flying near them. There's so much traffic around airports these days that weaving through this area can be like flying through a shooting gallery. It takes every ounce of concentration from both the pilot and copilot to make sure some small plane doesn't stray unintentionally into your flight path. Fortunately, we fly that low only on takeoff and landing.

*"You mean the pilots have to keep an eye on all those small planes at the same time all this stick business and switch flipping is going on?"*

Yes, but that's why the Federal Aviation Administration exists. It's the job of the FAA to regulate airports and airspace so that the air traffic controllers can keep planes out of each other's way. But pilots still need to be alert—just in case—so the FAA also regulates the number of hours a commercial airline pilot can fly. Generally, that's about eighty hours per month, which is only about half the time most people work in regular jobs. Pilots need to be as relaxed and as awake as possible.

*"If it's so important to see what's going on outside, why is the windshield so small? You'd think we could have a better view."*

Actually, the windshield gives you the best view possible. Understand that there's a lot of glare in the full sun above the clouds, and cutting down the size of the windshield cuts down on the glare. You see, the engineers have a reason for just about everything.

*"I never knew that a simple airplane windshield could be so complicated."*

A lot of thought and careful design went into that windshield. See the six separate panes? Each one is 2 inches thick, and each has two separate heating grids built into it. There's one on the inside that works like a defroster in a car to evaporate cockpit moisture and another on the outside to prevent icing.

*"That's a pretty complicated window."*

You bet. A single pane costs as much as a BMW. And these windows are tough, too. They have to be, because as fast as we're moving, anything hitting us will have tremendous force. A bird can be like a bullet.

# THE TALE OF THE TAIL

As tall as a six-story building and as wide as a very wide thing, the tail of the 747-400 is a colossal piece of machinery. But the pilot can adjust its rudder or whale tail-like elevators at just the slight nudge of the control yoke—as though the tail were made out of paper instead of advanced aluminum alloys.

To move these mammoth control surfaces so easily, the 747 uses hydraulics. A hydraulic system is a network of tubing containing fluid kept under high pressure (about 3,000 pounds per square inch). It connects the controls to the control surfaces, such as the ailerons on the wing and the elevators on the tail. It uses the physics of pressure to translate and magnify force, so that a pilot's foot pressure on a rudder pedal can become powerful enough to move the 705-pound rudder.

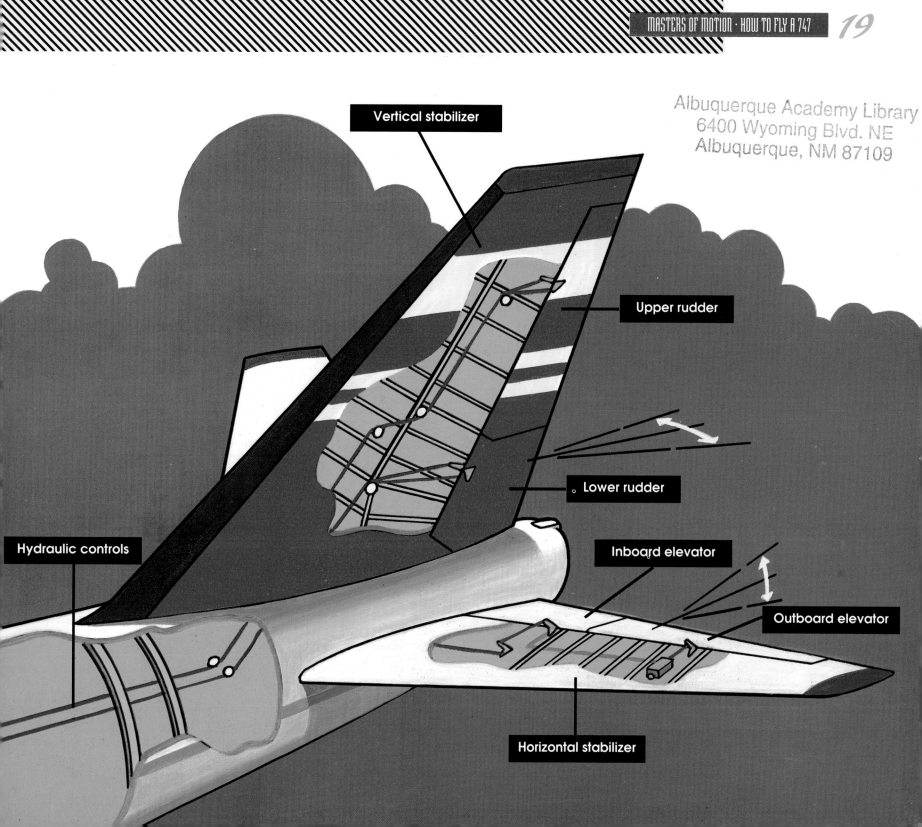

Vertical stabilizer

Upper rudder

Lower rudder

Hydraulic controls

Inboard elevator

Outboard elevator

Horizontal stabilizer

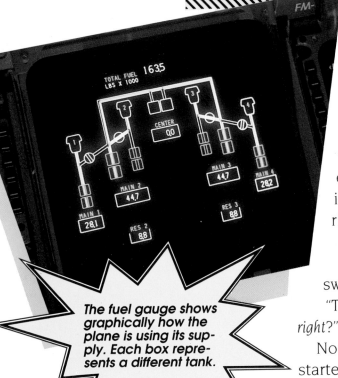

FM—

TOTAL FUEL 1635
LBS X 1000

CENTER
00

MAIN 2
447

MAIN 3
447

MAIN 4
282

MAIN 1
281

RES 2
88

RES 3
88

**The fuel gauge shows graphically how the plane is using its supply. Each box represents a different tank.**

"There's a voice in my ear now telling me we're cleared for takeoff."

That's the tower, so let's get a move on. We don't want to lose our takeoff slot. Are the flaps extended? The flap control is the little stick just to the right of the thrust levers.

"Got it. Flaps extended."

Are all four engines switched on?

"The switches are on the ceiling, right?"

No, those are the engine starters. The ones that matter now are the fuel control switches just below the throttle. I say, "Fuel control switches." And you say, "Forward and latched." Ready?

"You bet."

Fuel control switches.

"Forward and latched."

Now move the switch at that display in the middle of the control panel—it's called the EICAS, which stands for Engine Indication and Crew Alerting System—until you get to the engine display. There it is! That diagram shows all four engines running, each at 30 percent of capacity. Now turn the switch on the right side of the overhead panelmarked PASS TEMP.

"What's it for? Hey! What's that weird sound?"

That's just the air-conditioning system turning on. Without climate control, it gets pretty cold at 35,000 feet. More than fifty below, to be exact, and that's Centigrade, not Fahrenheit. It's like being at the top of the tallest mountain you can imagine—and then jumping about 10,000 feet straight up. The atmosphere is so thin at high altitudes that it doesn't provide much insulation from the icy cold of space. And there isn't much oxygen up there either. That's why we pressurize the inside of the plane before we take off. Otherwise, there wouldn't be enough air for everyone to breathe, and we'd all black out long before we reached our cruising altitude of 35,000 feet.

In fact, speaking of high altitudes, it's time to throw that little switch on the side panel. That's the "dead dog" switch.

# OVERROTATION

*"The dead dog switch? You've got to be kidding!"*

Do I sound like I'm kidding? The dead dog switch is a very important control.

*"One of the 365 most important?"*

That's right. We don't have room for useless switches in this cockpit. The dead dog is important because it turns on the heat in the cargo hold. If we didn't heat the hold, then the intense cold at high altitudes would kill all the animals we were transporting. The hold is always pressurized, but it's only heated when the dead dog switch is on.

*"Gotcha. Dead dog on. What about fuel? It's not like we're going to find any gas stations up there."*

Flip the EICAS again until you've called up the fuel display. Stop. That's it, the diagram that looks like a spider. Each box shows the status of a different fuel tank, and the lines connecting the boxes represent the fuel lines connecting the tanks to the engines. Problems with the fuel lines show up in red on the display.

*"So we have a full load of fuel, and the lines are all functioning properly. Can we take off now?"*

You bet. Take it away. Just remember to pull back gently on the stick as the speed reaches VR. You only need to bring the nose up about 10 degrees for a proper climbing angle. Anything more than 12 degrees may cause overrotation, which means that we might drag the tail on the ground or stall because the angle of attack is too great to achieve lift.

*"And that would be bad."*

Yes, that would be very bad.

*"How do I tell when I've got the proper climb angle?"*

You watch the wing display on the PFD, you remember, the Primary Flight Display. In addition to showing roll, those sideways L's also move up and down to show pitch. The horizontal hash marks give you the angle measures. And I mean pull back gently. With all the thrust you have, it's surprisingly easy to overrotate.

*"All right, I'm increasing power now. Brakes off. Thrust levers to maximum power. We're moving! Here we go!"*

The takeoff run. A 747 pilot views the runway from the height of a bedroom window in a three-story house.

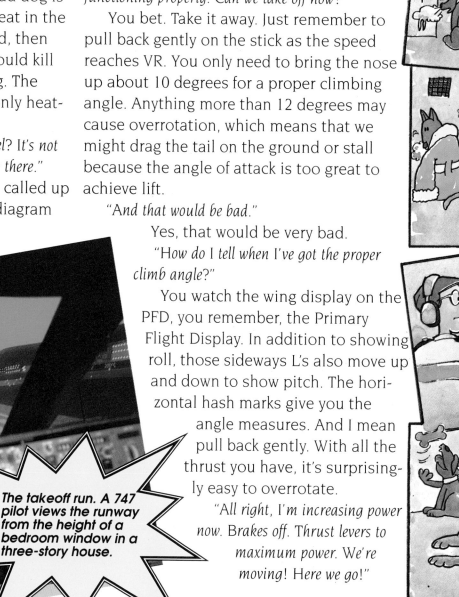

## TAKEOFF

Varoom! There's so much power here, all in the palm of my hand. When I just pushed those levers forward, I could really feel the kick. The acceleration pushed me back so far in my seat, it's a good thing it's padded!

The plane is picking up speed now as more than 400 tons of metal and machine rumble down the runway. Outside the engines are roaring, but inside the cockpit, it's remarkably quiet. The runway lights are whipping by. Up here on the flight deck, right on the nose of this monster, in a tiny cabin no more than nine feet across, I feel like a pimple on the nose of a charging rhinoceros. Faster and faster we go. One hundred knots. One hundred ten. One hundred twenty. There's V1, and I'm beginning to see the red lights that signal the end of the runway. One hundred thirty. One hundred forty. That's it—VR—and I'm pulling back ever so gently on the stick. The nose is coming up quickly. More angle of attack, so more lift. The PFD shows 10 degrees, 12 degrees, 14 degrees. I feel as though I'm being separated from my stomach.

The plane is swooping up into the air, much faster than I expected, and we're climbing. There's the bump of the landing gear. Five hundred feet, a thousand. The flaps retract. Two thousand feet, five thousand. In

> The thrust that comes from just one modern 747-400 engine is greater than the combined thrust—56,000 pounds—of the four-engine 707-120.

# A LOT OF HOT AIR

Three hundred years ago, Sir Isaac Newton had a bright idea. For every action, he suggested, there had to be an equal and opposite reaction. Today's jet engines are based on this simple principle, now known as Newton's Third Law of Motion. The action is the expulsion of a jet of air out the back of each engine. The reaction is the equal and opposite force that pushes the engine, and the plane to which it is attached, forward.

As a jet flies through the sky, air naturally passes through its engines. Most of that air continues on its way along the inside of the bypass ducts, cooling and muffling the engine. But some of the air is channeled into the engine's compressors by the turbofan—a shaft with fan blades that rotates like a turbine, hence its name. Once the air is compressed by the turbofan, it enters a combustion chamber where burning fuel heats it, causing the air to expand and be emitted from the engine as a jet of hot, high-pressure gas. This jet is the engine's thrust, which is controlled by the throttle in the cockpit. The throttle manages the engine's thrust by regulating the amount of fuel delivered to the combustion chamber.

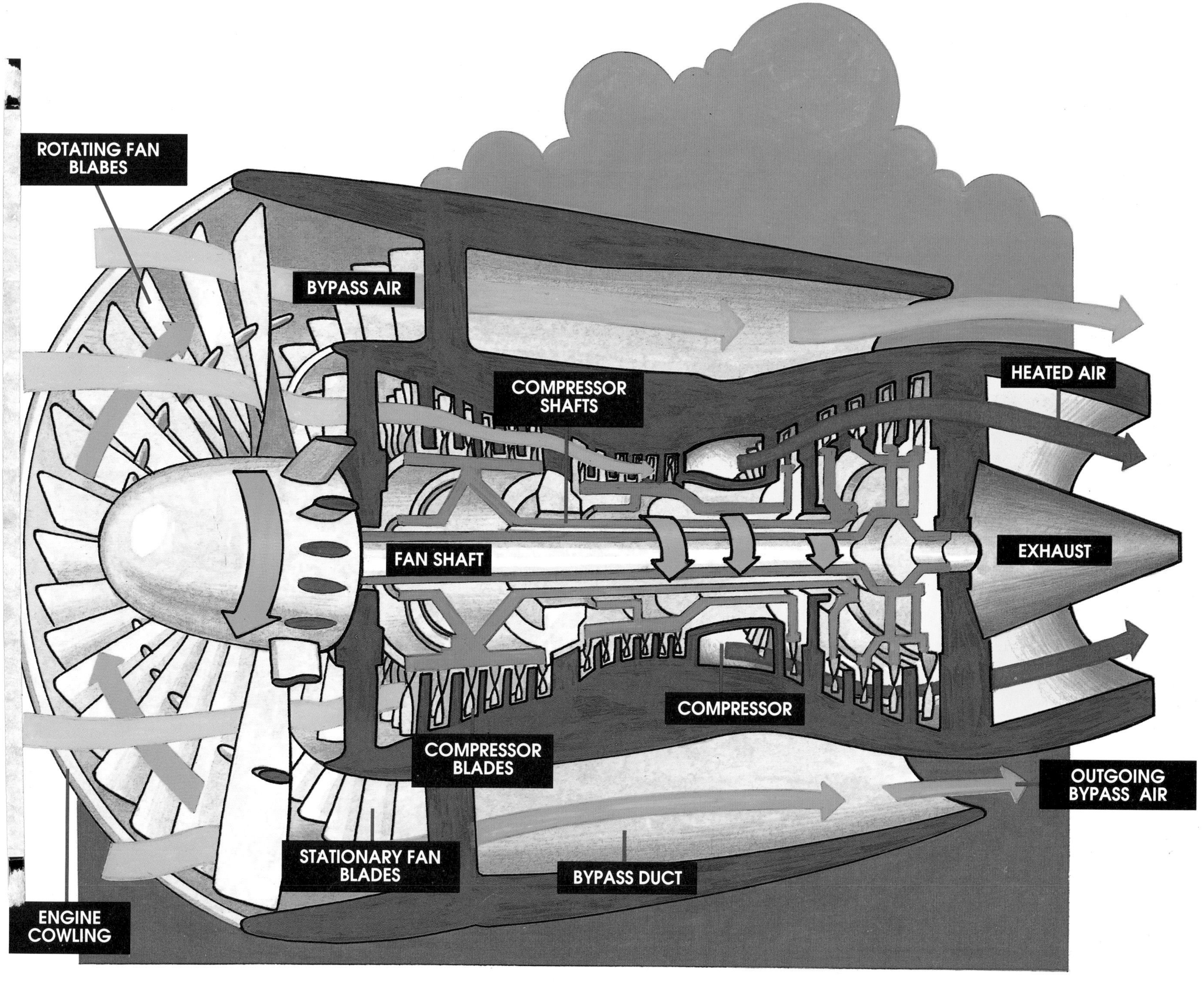

ROTATING FAN BLABES

BYPASS AIR

COMPRESSOR SHAFTS

HEATED AIR

FAN SHAFT

EXHAUST

COMPRESSOR

COMPRESSOR BLADES

STATIONARY FAN BLADES

BYPASS DUCT

OUTGOING BYPASS AIR

ENGINE COWLING

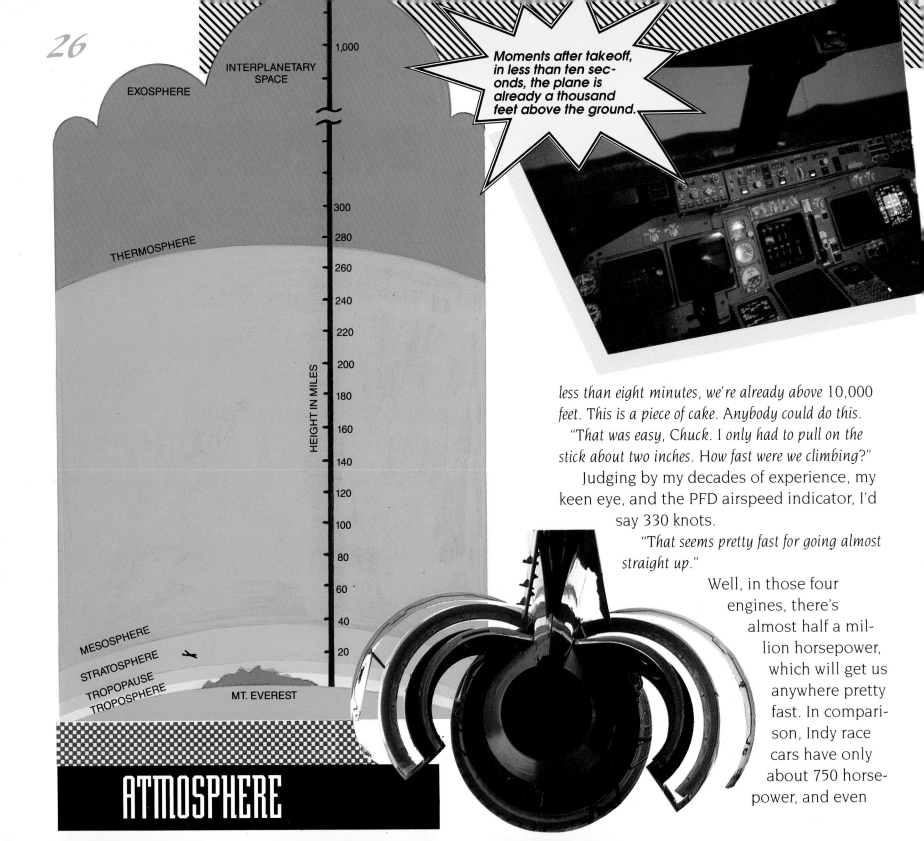

EXOSPHERE

INTERPLANETARY SPACE

THERMOSPHERE

1,000

300
280
260
240
220
200
180
160
140
120
100
80
60
40
20

HEIGHT IN MILES

MESOSPHERE
STRATOSPHERE
TROPOPAUSE
TROPOSPHERE

MT. EVEREST

# ATMOSPHERE

**Moments after takeoff, in less than ten seconds, the plane is already a thousand feet above the ground.**

*less than eight minutes, we're already above 10,000 feet. This is a piece of cake. Anybody could do this.*

"That was easy, Chuck. I only had to pull on the stick about two inches. How fast were we climbing?"

Judging by my decades of experience, my keen eye, and the PFD airspeed indicator, I'd say 330 knots.

"That seems pretty fast for going almost straight up."

Well, in those four engines, there's almost half a million horsepower, which will get us anywhere pretty fast. In comparison, Indy race cars have only about 750 horsepower, and even

America's early space rockets had only one quarter the horsepower of a 747-400.

*"Check."*

That's Chuck.

*"I meant Roger."*

Who's Roger?

*"Never mind."*

## IN FLIGHT

O.K., level off when you get to 35,000 feet. We can go as high as 45,000, but you wouldn't want to cruise that high. The air's pretty thin up there.

*"Is that a problem?"*

Think about lift again. Remember that it comes from the difference in air pressure above and below the wing. If you take away some of that air, which is what happens at high altitudes, you reduce the difference and therefore the lift as well. Basically, there are not enough air molecules up there to support the weight of a 747. That's why there's a limit to how high planes can fly.

*"Can any planes fly higher than a 747?"*

Well, fighter jets can because they're lighter and faster. Their streamlined shape and powerful engines allow them to fly at speeds surpassing Mach 2, or twice the speed of sound. More air passes under their wings in a given time, which means more air molecules for support and also greater lift.

*"Talking about speed, let's see just how fast this bird can travel. I'll push forward on the thrusters and—hey, they're already as far forward as they can go! Does that mean we can't fly any faster?"*

We certainly won't get any more thrust, that's for sure. Having all four engines at full throttle means the 747 is generating as much thrust as it can. But speed isn't simply dependent on thrust. Drag must also be taken into account. Right now, because we're climbing, the high angle of attack we're using to increase lift is also increasing the plane's drag. When we level off in a minute, we'll encounter a lot less wind resistance. Less drag, less resistance, more air-speed. O.K., level off now.

*"Leveling off. Hey, I can already feel us speeding up! It's almost like another takeoff. I feel the acceleration pushing me back in my seat again."*

Look at the Primary Flight

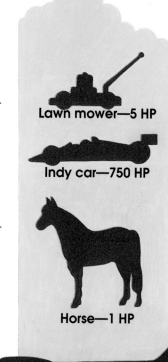

Lawn mower—5 HP

Indy car—750 HP

Horse—1 HP

747—500,000 HP

Locomotive—40,000 HP

Car—200 HP

GREAT FLIGHT!

L.A. TO St. LOUIS IN RECORD TIME!

MORE HORSEPOWER!

The giant pieces of the 747 are actually moved from one work station to the next on a cushion of air.

# BUILDING THE PERFECT BEAST

Over 75,000 engineering drawings as well as more than 12,000 hours of wind tunnel tests went into the design of the first 747. An entirely new engine had to be developed to power the largest plane the world had ever seen. And as though that weren't enough, building the first 747 presented an additionally awesome task for Boeing, requiring the construction of the largest enclosed space in the world, the 747 factory in Everett, Washington.

Today's 747-400 is made up of more than six million individual parts that are shipped to Everett from all over the world. Five planes a month roll off the assembly lines that cover a total of 43 acres—more than forty football fields—of factory floor. The power needed to light the factory would light the equivalent of 32,000 average American homes.

Early on, the skeleton of the fuselage—the central, tubular section of the plane—is placed within some giant revolving scaffolding that supports it while the metal sheets that form its skin are attached. Then the fuselage is moved to the beginning of the assembly line proper, where more sections are added including the wings, nose, and tail.

As these sections are bolted together, assembly line workers also add the muscles of the plane, the hydraulic systems that operate the control surfaces. Two thousand pieces of tubing, through which a fluid is pumped under pressure, serve to control the 747's ailerons, flaps, landing gear, and other moving parts.

The nervous system of the plane is added at this time—its electrical wiring. The electrical system carries the pilot's commands to every part of the vessel and also relays information from the various sensors and gauges on board. Every system on the plane, from the landing gear to the cargo doors, is monitored electronically by lights and indicators on the plane's control panel.

Display. See the pitch line? The one you used to check your nose angle on takeoff? It's down under 2 degrees now, which is a much speedier angle of attack.

*"I've never seen clouds move by so fast. The PFD says we're doing Mach .84—almost the speed of sound."*

That's about 495 knots, or 570 miles per hour.

*"Can we go any faster?"*

We can, but we wouldn't want to. The plane tends to shake a lot—and if we go fast enough, it could eventually shake apart.

*"And that would be bad."*

Yes, very bad.

*"O.K., I think I'll pass on that. But tell me, how slow can the 747 go? I mean, that can't be too dangerous."*

Actually, going too slow can be just as dangerous as going too fast. But the 747 is such a safe plane that you don't really have to worry too much. Even if you were to stall, the plane would try to right itself.

Technically, a stall is what happens when a plane's airspeed becomes so low that its wings no longer generate enough lift to keep it aloft. At first, the nose goes up, but then the angle of attack becomes too steep, and you stall. We can try a stall if you'd like.

# THE SPEED OF SOUND

How fast is the speed of sound, otherwise known as Mach 1? Well, that depends. In fact, it depends on temperature. At 0°C (or 32°F), the speed of sound is about 740 miles per hour. As the temperature goes up or down, however, so does the speed of sound. A convenient formula is:

Speed of sound = 740 mi./hr. + (1.3)(temperature in °C)

At -45°C (the temperature of the lower stratosphere), the speed of sound would therefore be approximately 682 miles per hour. This means that if you and I were standing 682 miles apart in -45°C weather, and you shouted to me, I would hear you exactly one hour later, give or take a few seconds. But you'd have to shout very loud.

*"It's not dangerous?"*

No, not really. Once a plane is flying, it wants to keep flying. And the way 747s are built—well, let's just do it, and you'll see. Go ahead. Pull back on the throttle. That'll slow us down.

*"You're right, the nose is dropping, and the tail is coming up. Wow! It seems as though we've almost stopped in midair! But wait, now we're starting to slide forward. What do I do now!?"*

Relax. Just let the plane take over. See how it evens out? We've dropped about 2,000 feet, but the nose has come down and we're starting to fall into a glide. Now just ease forward on the thrust levers a bit, and we'll be cruising again.

*"That was fantastic, but I'd feel a little better if we got back some of that altitude. I just pull back on the stick, right?"*

That's right. Anything else you'd like to try while we're up here? The sky's the limit.

*"Well, Chuck, now that I've found out how fast—and how slow—the 747 can go, I think I'd like to learn how it turns."*

No problem. Just take a look out the window there. See anything familiar?

*"Why, Chuck, it looks like the World Trade Center!"*

That's right. Of course, we wouldn't normally fly this low in a

The World Trade Center is normally avoided both night and day by commercial aircraft.

# WORLD TRADE CENTER

747. But like I said, for you the sky's the limit. I'll clear the airspace, so why don't you fly in for a closer look. Take a spin around the block. I think you'll find the 747 corners pretty well for a big bird.

*"What do I do? Use the steering wheel? I mean, the stick?"*

Turning the control yoke to the right and left raises and lowers the ailerons on the wings. But you also use the pedals. They control the rudder, remember.

*"O.K., so if I turn the wheel to the right and press the right pedal..."*

Then you turn right.

*"But what's actually happening?"*

A number of things, all of which help the plane turn. Pressing the right pedal swivels the rudder to the right, which has the effect of concentrating the force of the wind on the right side of the plane. This causes the tail section to swing left, and as the plane pivots, the nose comes right.

Turning the control yoke to the right lowers the aileron on the left wing and raises the aileron on the right wing. Now think about what that does to the airflow over the wings. What do you think happens when the right aileron goes up? Do you think the right wing rises or drops?

*"Drops?"*

You're right on the money, because raising the aileron interrupts the flow of air over the wing. It causes the air to move slower and more erratically, thereby reducing the pressure differential and also the lift. The same principle happens in reverse when you lower an aileron.

*"I think I understand. The lowered aileron concentrates more air under the wing, which increases the pressure differential, so you get more lift."*

Bingo. So the right wing goes down, the left wing comes up, and you bank into the turn as the rudder pivots the plane.

*"And when I turn the wheel to the left..."*

Then your left wing comes down, your right wing comes up, and you turn left—as long as you're also giving it some left pedal. Before we start turning, though, it might be a good idea for you to check the altitude. The World Trade Center is about 1,350 feet tall, and the altimeter says—

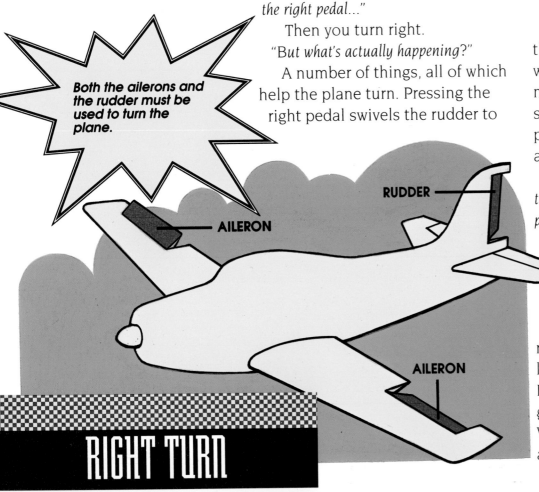

**Both the ailerons and the rudder must be used to turn the plane.**

RUDDER

AILERON

AILERON

# RIGHT TURN

## PROJECTORS
Three high-tech color projectors are used to generate the simulator's computer-controlled visuals. Each one projects a different section of the simulated landscape, and these sections overlap to create a truly panoramic scene. Helicopter simulators use five projectors to display an even wider view.

## PILOT'S VIEW
The projectors are focused onto a screen from which the images are then reflected onto a curved mirror that wraps all the way around the flight deck windows. Using a mirror gives the pilots the impression they are looking off into infinity rather than at a movie.

## PROGRAMMER'S STATION
Behind the pilot's seat is a computer console at which the simulator programmer sits. Using this console, the programmer can control all the different simulation variables—changing the visuals from day to night, for example, at the flip of a switch. The programmer can also record a pilot's performance during a simulated flight and play it back later for review.

# FLYING ON THE GROUND

Almost soon as there were planes, people began looking for a cheaper, safer way of training pilots than putting them into the air. But how to do it? The answer was the flight simulator.

The first simulators were little more than very large barrels that could be tipped in different directions by a system of wires and pulleys. Today, however, simulators are $24 million machines that replicate every aspect of flying exactly. Giant jacks under the simulator heave it to and fro if a hurricane simulation is called for, while a highly advanced projection system displays very convincing three-dimensional thunderheads just outside the cockpit window.

Projected onto a large, wraparound screen, the computer-generated images provide a field of vision that stretches all the way around the cockpit. Wherever the pilot looks, there's a realistic landscape, or city, or weather system, to actually fly around in. Other effects—like turbulence, wind, and rain—are provided by a computer program designed to resemble the random effects of these weather conditions. In this way, no one, not even the simulator programmer, knows what will happen next.

The simulator is such a realistic and effective learning tool that many pilots today have more experience on the simulator than they do on the plane itself. Every control response is so carefully reproduced that pilots truly get a sense of what it's like to fly a 747. The only difference between a simulated flight and a real one is that no one's safety is at stake.

A HURRICANE

"I guess I better pull up a bit."

Otherwise your wing might hit the towers as you turn.

"And that would be bad."

Yes, that would be very bad. I try to keep an open mind at all times, but I can safely say that avoiding buildings is generally a good idea.

"Well, since we're in agreement on that, here goes the turn."

Incredible! I'm so close I can see in the windows! And turning isn't that difficult, either. I feel as though I'm riding an 870,000-pound skateboard that flies! Banking tilts the plane about 30 degrees, and I can feel a slight slipping and sliding as we scoot around the towers. There's that big hand pressing me into my seat again. And already we're back where we started. I'd better stop turning and level out.

Good job, junior birdman. Just check the attitude indicator on the PFD, though, to make sure you've leveled off. Great. What next?

"Gee, let me think. I guess a really steep dive is out of the question."

I wouldn't recommend it. Tendency to hit the ground, you know.

"And that would be—"

Bad. You have anything else in mind?

"How about night flying?"

No problem. Presto! It's nightfall.

"Yikes! How'd you do that?"

When you've been flying as long as I have, you learn a few tricks. And, like I said before, for you the sky's the limit.

O.K. Back to business. Look at your control displays. When you're flying at night, you really have to depend on your instruments. But we can switch to the autopilot if you'd like to take a break.

The 747 has the most sophisticated automatic pilot ever built. It's even more advanced than the one used in the space shuttle. In fact, in normal flight, especially at night, the plane is usually flown by the computer. The pilot and copilot just monitor the control displays—and look out the windows—to make sure everything's functioning properly. You can pretty much count on the autopilot to take care of all the routine tasks of flight, such as keeping the plane in the air and headed in the right direction at the proper speed. The autopilot can handle the plane from moments after takeoff right through to a landing, but the pilot still has to take off manually.

"You know, Chuck, this night flying is really pretty neat, but I think I'd like to try something a little more exciting. Tell me, what's a hurricane like?"

Why tell you when I can show you? Do me a favor. Keep flipping the Primary Flight Display until—there. Stop there. That's a radar map showing weather conditions for miles in every direction. Aha! We're in luck. There's a hurricane brewing just off the coast of South Carolina. Let's take it in.

"Hey, the plane's bucking already. It feels like we're riding over a bunch of potholes, but there's no street up here."

That's just turbulence. Nothing to worry

# REDUNDANCY AND THE 747

Safety has to play a key role in the game plan for any aircraft, especially one intended for commercial use. What if lightning strikes and the power goes out? What if an engine is lost? What if all four engines are lost? What if the control cable to the rudder snaps? These are all scenarios that the engineers at Boeing considered when they were designing the 747. Their solution? Redundancy.

Redundancy is the practice of backing up key systems, not once but many times. On a 747-400, for example, there are four separate hydraulic systems that can lower the landing gear. This way, if one system fails, the pilot can just flip a switch and fall back on the next one, and the next, and so on. Each hydraulic control system is run through a different part of the plane's airframe, so that damage to any one area won't cripple the plane. The same is true of the electrical system. There are 175 miles of wire in each 747 engine alone, and enough wire in the entire plane to go around the world three times! Most of this backup is the 747's insurance against disaster.

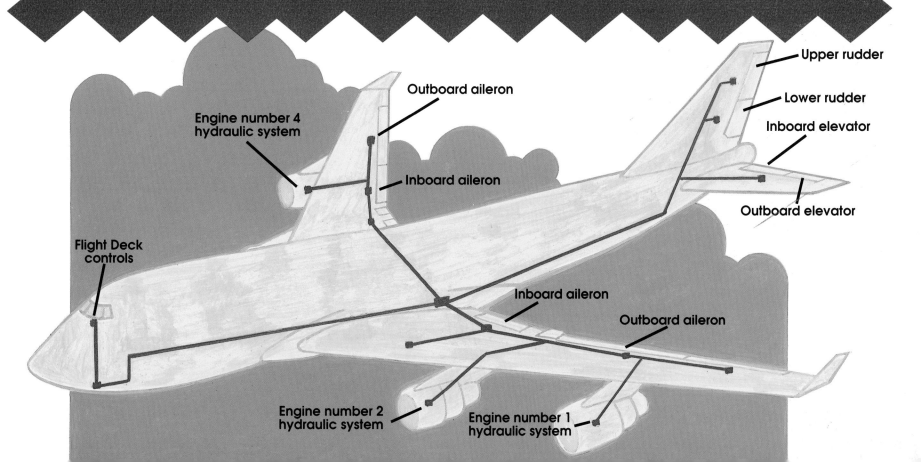

Upper rudder

Outboard aileron

Lower rudder

Inboard elevator

Engine number 4 hydraulic system

Inboard aileron

Outboard elevator

Flight Deck controls

Inboard aileron

Outboard aileron

Engine number 2 hydraulic system

Engine number 1 hydraulic system

# MICROBURSTS

Can rain be dangerous? You bet! Few weather conditions today pose a deadlier threat to air travel than the microburst, which is to normal rainfall what a fire hose is to a garden sprinkler. A microburst is a sudden, extremely powerful downpour that covers only a small patch of sky—but with an enormously concentrated force.

Until recently, microbursts existed only in theory. Some people suggested them as causes for accidents that were otherwise unexplainable, but there was no hard evidence. Not until Dr. Theodore Fujita of the University of Chicago examined photos taken at the site of a major rainstorm in West Virginia. In these photos, Fujita found concentrations of trees that had been crushed from above, as though they'd been stepped on by a giant foot! Fujita became convinced the damage had been caused by microbursts, and he eventually managed to convince the National Weather Service as well. As a result of Fujita's work, many airliners now carry onboard warning systems that monitor microburst activity and sound an alarm in the cockpit whenever one appears to be imminent.

about. But you see those red spots on the radar? Those are concentrated downpours. I'd avoid them.

"*What's happening now? I haven't pulled back on the stick, but I can feel us rising and the altimeter says we're climbing at 100 feet per second!*"

Don't worry. You often catch updrafts in thunderheads like this one. But watch out for the downdraft that usually follows. The plane can handle this kind of weather, but you generally want to avoid it when you can. The ups and downs aren't very good for anyone's stomach, and the hail you often find in these thunderheads can do millions of dollars in damage.

Right now, though, all we can do is fly through it. So keep the attitude level and the bearing steady.

"*What was that flash?*"

Lightning, of course, but I wouldn't worry too much about it. There are protective systems built into the body of the plane that can take care of stray bolts.

"*Shouldn't I try to fly around it?*"

As I said, it's generally a good idea to fly around areas of bad weather, but once you're in them, there's not much you can do. You can try flying around the lightning if you'd like, but I think you'll find that a bit too tricky. In fact, some engineers have told me that all the electronics in this plane actually attract the lightning.

*"So it's harmless?"*

Well, not totally. A typical lightning bolt carries about 200,000 amperes of electrical current, which is enough to power 2,000 homes. And that much juice can really play havoc with a plane's electrical system if it hits in the wrong place. You can see how important the electrical system is—it powers all the control displays, the guidance system, the autopilot—so you do want to be careful with it.

*"If lightning can foul up an electrical system, even with all the safeguards, why isn't it considered a more serious threat?"*

Because there isn't just one electrical system on this plane. We've got at least four of them. If one goes, then another takes over automatically.

*"Have you ever been hit by lightning?"*

Not really, but I did pass through some St. Elmo's fire once. That's an unusual sort of lightning that clings to the wings and cockpit of the plane and even comes into the cabin sometimes. I once saw a ball of it come into the cockpit, roll down the aisle, and leave through the tail section. It was quite a sight, like glowing swamp gas. The flames dance round like blazes, and the electrical system goes wild. But it passes soon enough. Looks like we're through the hurricane now.

*"Great. I think I could use some different weather for a while, something a bit calmer."*

How about some fog? I'll bet we can find some in Seattle. Let me work a little more magic, and here we are in the Pacific Northwest. I was right. There's about 500 feet of fog stacked on the ground here.

*"I can see the Space Needle on the left and Mount Rainier over on the right. But I sure can't see any airport or a runway."*

The Seattle Space Needle and Mt. Rainier viewed from a flight simulator.

Believe me, there's one down there. But in this soup, you'd have to land on instruments, and I think it's better for you to see what you're doing.

*"So where do we land?"*

I'd say Hong Kong is the place. Just take a left at Mount Rainier. But it's a bit of a ride across the Pacific, so let's engage the IRS.

*"What's the IRS?"*

The Inertial Reference System. It gives navigational directions to the autopilot. You see that keypad to your right, just in front of the throttle? You punch a set of coordinates into that panel, and the IRS, working with the autopilot, takes you where you want to go automatically.

*"Where do the coordinates come from?"*

They're calculated from your flight plan. Ground control gives them to you before you take off so you can program them into the IRS while you're still on the runway. That way, the autopilot always knows where you're going.

*"But how does the plane even know where it is?"*

The most important part of the IRS is its tracking system. Ships navigate by a series of positional calculations. They use landmarks or the stars to figure out where they are, as well as a compass to tell them their bearing. But the IRS works a different way. When you begin a flight, all you have to do is tell the IRS where it is. From then on, it keeps track.

*"I'm not sure I follow."*

Well, let's say you're standing on Fourth Street, and you walk four blocks. You don't need to see a street sign to know that you're now standing on Eighth Street. The IRS works on the same principle. The coordinates you punch in are like directions: travel for so long at such-and-such a speed, then turn north 5 degrees, then go 200 miles and turn 7 degrees south southeast. Then descend 2,000 feet. The IRS remembers how far and in which direction—right or left, up or down—the plane travels. Then it calculates where the plane is by adding up all the movements made during flight. It also accounts for such things as the effects of wind resistance, wind drift, even the changing weight of the plane as fuel is consumed or ice accumulates. The IRS is so accurate that it can take a 747 within 200 meters of where you want it to go. It can even land the plane.

*"So I can just sit back and relax? You know, Chuck, flying isn't too tough at all once you understand how to use the autopilot."*

You can relax if you want to. The autopilot will take us right into our landing approach.

*"Is that Hong Kong down there?"*

That's right. Time to land.

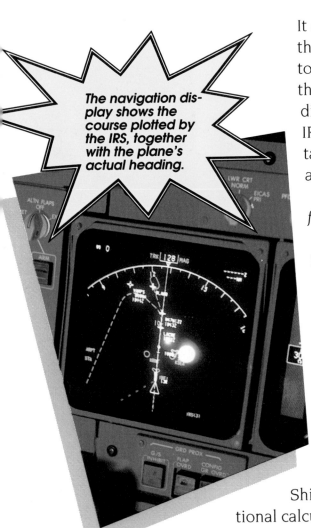

**The navigation display shows the course plotted by the IRS, together with the plane's actual heading.**

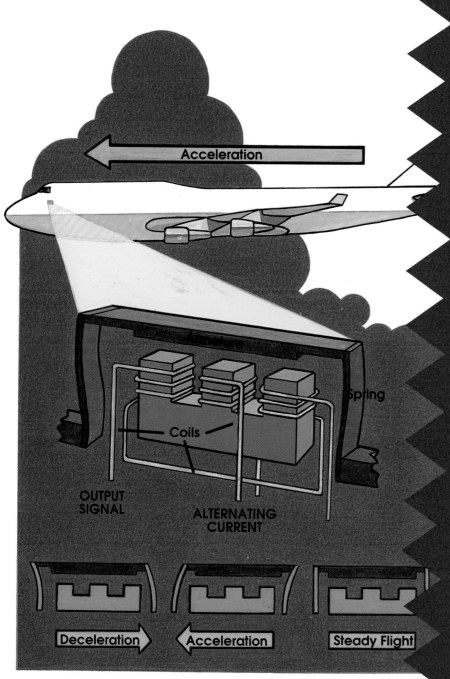

Acceleration

Armature

Spring

Coils

OUTPUT
SIGNAL

ALTERNATING
CURRENT

Deceleration

Acceleration

Steady Flight

# LOOK, MA, NO PILOT!

The Inertial Reference System of the 747 uses a simple idea to perform an extremely complicated task. The basic building block of the IRS is a gauge called the accelerometer, which detects changes in the plane's flight path. Originally, accelerometers were electric coils set inside springs. Changes in the plane's direction caused the electric coil to move against the spring, which triggered electronic signals to the flight computer. Today's accelerometers use lasers instead.

The IRS of the 747 is composed of three accelerometers measuring east-west, north-south, and vertical changes in flight, respectively. When an accelerometer measures a change because of drift or turbulence, the IRS directs the flight computer to make appropriate course adjustments.

To calculate airspeed and altitude, the IRS uses devices called pressure instruments. Airspeed is measured by a pitot tube, which is a tube bent at a right angle that measures the velocity of the air passing through it. Altitude is calculated from barometric pressure readings—the lower the pressure, the higher the altitude above sea level. Barometric altitude is accurate enough at cruising altitudes, but on landings it is supplemented by a radar signal aimed straight down that yields the exact height of the plane above the ground.

Taken together, the laser accelerometers and the pressure instruments give the IRS an unbelievable degree of accuracy. With human beings doing little more than punching in coordinates, the Inertial Reference System of a 747 can take its passengers and crew to within 200 meters of their destination!

**The landing approach at Hong Kong's International Airport can be difficult for beginners.**

## LANDING

**W**hy don't you flip on the radio, and we'll get our approach information from the tower? The switch is on your right.

*"The tower says they're picking us up."*

That means they see us on their radar screens. The altitude they're giving you now is one that has been cleared for our plane. That way, there's much less danger of us running into anybody, especially once we're back under 10,000 feet—among all those small airplanes. O.K., soon we'll switch off the IRS, but first let's program in the approach information.

*"Program programmed."*

Cute, kid. Now, listen. To land, you essentially take off in reverse. Put the landing gear down. Extend the flaps. Switch the autopilot to landing mode, and steer the plane according to the line behind what used to be the navigation display. That shows you the proper glide path, which the IRS has conveniently displayed for us from information sent by ground transmitters. Make sure that little plane symbol stays right on it.

*"What's the glide path?"*

It's the best possible approach for the runway we'll be landing on, and it takes into account a constant 3 degree descent angle, which is called the "glide slope." Ease off on the thrusters to bring down your airspeed. Gravity will pull us down naturally. You won't have to push the stick forward at all.

From 1,500 feet on down, you'll be traveling at V-Thresh, or velocity threshold, which is typically 20 to 30 percent faster than stall speed. Practically, that's about 115 to 140 knots. Then, once we're on the ground, pull the throttle all the way back. There's only one runway in Hong Kong, and it's surrounded by a city, so we have to stop quickly.

"How tough is it?"

Actually, it's probably one of the toughest heavy transport runways in the world. But don't worry. No problem. Just remember that in the cockpit we're 29 feet above the landing gear. That means we'll set down a little bit before you expect.

"Where are the brakes?"

They're on the rudder pedals. You push at the top of them, and that applies the brakes. But you need a lot more than brakes to stop a 747. Fortunately, the wings have been designed to do a lot of work for you. Vertical flaps called spoilers pop up just as you land, and they break the airflow over the wing, clamping the plane to the ground and killing the lift that might otherwise cause you to pick up again. And you've also got thrust reversers. These are doors in the engines that close, diverting the jet thrust forward and slowing the forward momentum of the plane.

"Hey, Chuck! We're swaying out of the glide path!"

Just relax. Give it some right rudder. Raise your nose a bit. What's your speed?

"One hundred forty knots. But are you sure that's fast enough? The airport's still so far away. It looks like we're going to land in the ocean!"

One hundred forty is fine. It's a lot faster than you think, and the flaps will keep us up. Hold on, we're almost in.

Hold on! This is pretty scary. I can feel the whole plane shudder from side to side at just the slightest touch of the control yoke. My fingers are getting stiff now. I've got to relax, but I'm sweating so much that it feels like a furnace in here. This cockpit has turned into a very lonely place. Where's the glide path? It's on the Primary Flight Display. Good. Just keep the little plane even with that little line, and the big plane stays even with the big runway. Here it comes! Look out below! And there it is. The bump. Throttle back. Spoilers up. Thrust reversers. All right! We're down! What a landing!

Great job. Hardly a bump. But let's also pull up on the brakes now. Those red lights mean we're getting to the end of the runway pretty fast. Good. Excellent. Well done. I don't know whether you're ready to solo yet, but I think overall you did a quite creditable job with the big bird. By the way, did I ever tell you that the 747-400 is the largest commercial aircraft in the world?

# GLOSSARIZED INDEX

**accelerometer**—a measuring device in the Inertial Reference System that detects changes in a plane's flight path, 41

**ailerons**—surfaces on a plane's wings that control roll, 7, 15, 32

**angle of attack**—the angle at which the wings meet the relative wind, 4-6, 24, 27-28

**attitude**—the relative orientation of a plane, 7

**autopilot**—a computer capable of flying a plane, 6, 35, 40-41, 42

**barometric altitude**—a plane's height above sea level, 8, 41

**cockpit controls,** 6-13, 20-21, 27-32

**Cockpit Voice Recorder**—the "black box" that records everything said in the cockpit, 17

**control surfaces**—surfaces on the wings and tail that control a plane's movement, 7, 10, 12-15, 18-19, 30-32, 43

**dead dog switch**—the switch that turns on heat in the cargo hold, 20-21

**drag**—the resistance to thrust caused by friction between the air and the plane, 8-9, 27

**Engine Indication and Crew Alerting System (EICAS),** 20-21

**elevators**—surfaces on a plane's tail that control pitch, 7, 12-13

**flaps**—control surfaces on a plane's wings used in takeoff and landing, 8, 14-15, 42

**flight simulator,** 33

**fuselage**—the central, tubular section of a plane, 9, 29

**glide path**—the approach to a runway landing, 42-43

**glide slope**—the descent angle for a glide path, 43

**hydraulics**—a network of tubing containing pressurized fluid by which the cockpit controls manipulate the plane's control surfaces, 18

**Inertial Reference System (IRS),** 40-42

**jet engine,** 24-27, 43

**knot**—a measure of speed equal to one nautical mile per hour, 12

**landing,** 42-43

**lift**—the upward force that keeps a plane aloft, 3-6, 27, 32

**Mach number**—a measure of speed relative to the speed of sound, 27-30

**nautical mile**—about 1.15 statute miles, 12

**pitch**—an aspect of attitude, 7, 21, 30

**pitot tube**—a device that measures the velocity of air passing through it, 41

**Primary Flight Display (PFD)**, 8-9, 21, 27-30, 35

**principles of flight**, 2-6, 32

**redundancy**—the use of backup systems, 37

**relative wind**—the speed of the air flowing past a plane's wings, 4

**roll**—an aspect of attitude, 7

**rudder**—surfaces on a plane's tail that control yaw, 7, 12-13, 18-19, 32

**size of a 747**, 2, 6

**speed of sound**, 27, 30

**spoilers**—control surfaces that break the airflow across the wings, 14-15, 43

**statute mile**—a regular mile (5,280 feet), 12

**taking off**, 6-14, 21-26

**thrust reversers**—doors in jet engines that divert thrust forward to slow down a plane on landing, 43

**transponder**—a radio transmitter, 17

**turning a 747**, 30-35

**yaw**—an aspect of attitude, 7

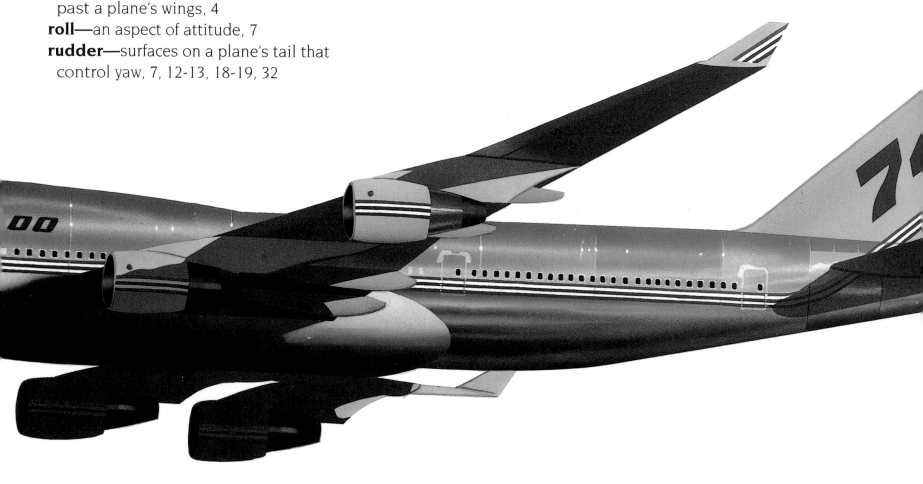

## X-ray Vision Series

Each title in the series is 8½" × 11", 48 pages, with four-color photographs and illustrations.

**Looking Inside the Brain**
Ron Schultz
$9.95 paper

**Looking Inside Cartoon Animation**
Ron Schultz
$9.95 paper

**Looking Inside Sports Aerodynamics**
Ron Schultz
$9.95 paper

## The Quill Hedgehog Adventures Series

*G*reen fiction for young readers. Each title in the series is written by John Waddington-Feather and illustrated by Doreen Edmond.

**Quill's Adventures in the Great Beyond**
*Book One*
5½" × 8½", 96 pages, $5.95 paper

**Quill's Adventures in Wasteland**
*Book Two*
5½" × 8½", 132 pages, $5.95 paper

**Quill's Adventures in Grozzieland**
*Book Three*
5½" × 8½", 132 pages, $5.95 paper

## Masters of Motion Series

Each title in the series is 10¼" × 9", 48 pages, with four-color photographs and illustrations.

**How to Drive an Indy Race Car**
David Rubel
$9.95 paper

**How to Fly a 747**
Tim Paulson
$9.95 paper

**How to Fly the Space Shuttle**
Russell Shorto
$9.95 paper   (avail. 11/92)

## The Extremely Weird Series

*A*ll of the titles in the Extremely Weird Series are written by Sarah Lovett, are 8½" × 11", 48 pages, and $9.95 paperbacks.

**Extremely Weird Bats**
**Extremely Weird Birds**
**Extremely Weird Endangered Species**
**Extremely Weird Fishes**
**Extremely Weird Frogs**
**Extremely Weird Insects**
**Extremely Weird Primates**
**Extremely Weird Reptiles**
**Extremely Weird Sea Creatures**
**Extremely Weird Spiders**

## Other Titles of Interest

**Kids Explore America's Hispanic Heritage**
Westridge Young Writers Workshop
7" × 9", 112 pages, illustrations
$7.95 paper

**Rads, Ergs, and Cheeseburgers**
*The Kids' Guide to Energy and the Environment*
Bill Yanda
*Illustrated by Michael Taylor*
7" × 9", 108 pages, two-color illustrations
$12.95 paper

**The Kids' Environment Book**
*What's Awry and Why*
Anne Pedersen
*Illustrated by Sally Blakemore*
7" × 9", 192 pages, two-color illustrations
$13.95 paper
For Ages 10 and Up

**The Indian Way**
*Learning to Communicate with Mother Earth*
Gary McLain
*Paintings by Gary McLain*
*Illustrations by Michael Taylor*
7" × 9", 114 pages, two-color illustrations
$9.95 paper

## The Kidding Around Travel Series

*A*ll of the titles listed below are 64 pages and $9.95 except for *Kidding Around the National Parks of the Southwest* and *Kidding Around Spain*, which are 108 pages and $12.95.

Kidding Around Atlanta
Kidding Around Boston
Kidding Around Chicago
Kidding Around the Hawaiian Islands
Kidding Around London
Kidding Around Los Angeles
Kidding Around the National Parks of the Southwest
Kidding Around New York City
Kidding Around Paris
Kidding Around Philadelphia
Kidding Around San Diego
Kidding Around San Francisco
Kidding Around Santa Fe
Kidding Around Seattle
Kidding Around Spain
Kidding Around Washington, D.C.